Mini Mammals

Mason Crest 6/07 18—

Text: Sharon Dalgleish
Consultant: George McKay, Conservation Biologist

This edition first published 2003 by
MASON CREST PUBLISHERS INC.
370 Reed Road
Broomall, PA 19008

© Weldon Owen Inc.
Conceived and produced by
Weldon Owen Pty Limited

Library of Congress Cataloging-in-Publication Data
on file at the Library of Congress
ISBN: 1-59084-193-X

Printed in Singapore.
1 2 3 4 5 6 7 8 9 06 05 04 03

CONTENTS

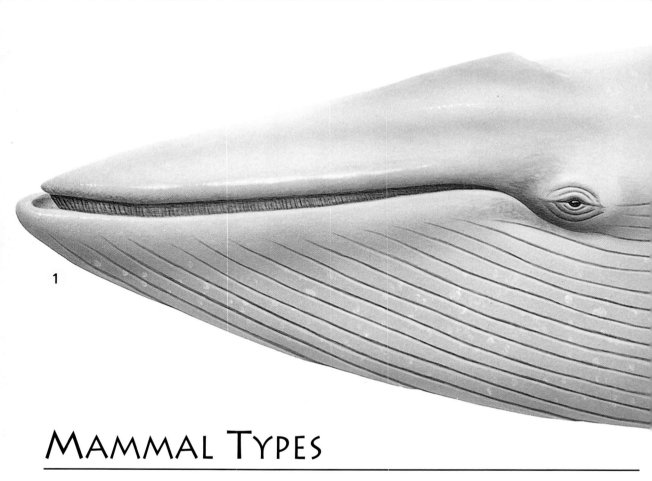

1

MAMMAL TYPES

Mammals come in an amazing range of body sizes and shapes. They live in every environment on Earth, except the very highest mountains and the frozen ice caps of Antarctica. The tiny field mouse is a mammal, and so is the enormous blue whale swimming in the ocean. Humans are mammals, too. The smaller the mammal, the faster its heartbeat. In one minute, an elephant's heart beats about 25 times. A human's heart beats about 65 times per minute.

1. blue whale
2. elephant
3. fruit bat
4. elk
5. hippopotamus
6. human
7. tiger
8. gorilla
9. kangaroo
10. armadillo
11. field mouse

OLD DOG

Cynognathus was a mammal-like reptile that lived 240 million years ago. Its name means "dog jaw."

IN THE BEGINNING

Many scientists believe the first mammals were small animals about 5 inches (12 centimeters) long. The modern platypus and echidna are related to these primitive mammals. When the dinosaurs died out 65 million years ago, mammals spread around the world and evolved into thousands of new species. In the picture, a female Arsinoitherium is defending her baby from a pack of predators on the plains of northern Africa, about 40 million years ago.

THE FIRST MAMMAL

Megazostrodon lived about 220 million years ago and is the oldest known mammal. It ate insects and probably laid eggs like an echidna.

SPIKY BEGINNINGS
Many scientists believe mammals slowly evolved from mammal-like reptiles such as this Dimetrodon.

MAMMAL SOCIETY

Most mammals are social and live together in groups. In a group, it is much easier to defend those who are younger or weaker. Mammals use smells, facial expressions, and body language to communicate with others in their group. They can warn of danger, or tell others they've found food. Dogs, for example, wag their tail when they are happy and snarl when they are angry.

PART OF A GROUP
Meerkats live together in packs.

PLAY TIME

Mammals look after their young for longer than most other animals. As these black bear cubs play, they will learn the skills they need to survive as adults.

DID YOU KNOW?

African vervet monkey "guards" use special calls to warn other members of the group when enemies such as leopards are nearby.

MORE FOR SHOW

Some male mammals fight to see which one will be the boss. These fights are mostly tests of strength, and don't usually cause serious injury.

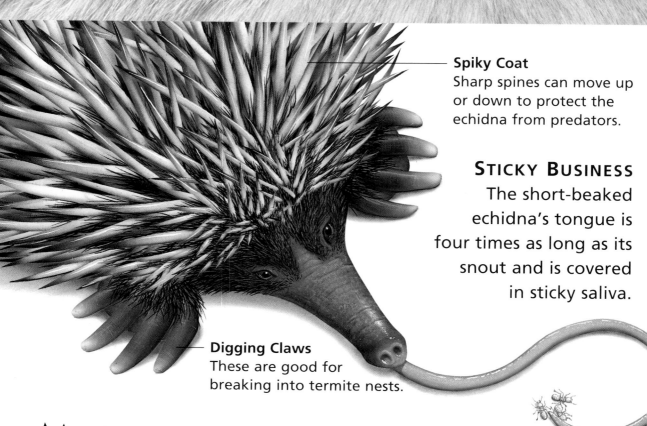

Spiky Coat
Sharp spines can move up
or down to protect the
echidna from predators.

STICKY BUSINESS
The short-beaked
echidna's tongue is
four times as long as its
snout and is covered
in sticky saliva.

Digging Claws
These are good for
breaking into termite nests.

MONOTREMES

Platypuses and echidnas are mammals that lay
eggs. They are called monotremes. Monotremes
have many of the reptilelike features of primitive
mammals. They have a lower body temperature
than other mammals, and echidnas hibernate in
winter. When an Australian platypus was first
sent to England in 1798, scientists thought it was
so strange, they believed it had to be a fake
made of different animals sewn together!

poisonous
spur

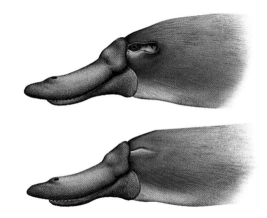

DID YOU KNOW?

On land, the platypus pulls back the webs on its front feet so it can use its claws to walk and dig burrows.

COVER UP

A fold of skin covers the platypus's eyes and ears when it dives. It uses its sensitive bill to find its way under water.

webbed front feet

SMOOTH SWIMMER

The platypus uses its powerful front feet for swimming. Its fur keeps it warm by holding a layer of air next to its skin.

CLIMBING KANGAROO

The tree kangaroo can climb straight up a tree by gripping with the claws of all four feet.

MARSUPIALS

Some mammals give birth to young that are not fully developed, but need to be protected in their mother's pouch until they can fend for themselves. These mammals with pouches are called marsupials. Marsupials live in many environments—in deserts and rain forests, in burrows and trees. They eat plants, insects, and meat. They glide, run, hop, climb, and swim to get around.

STRANGE BUT TRUE

The Tasmanian tiger was more like a marsupial wolf with a pouch than a tiger. The last known Tasmanian tiger died in 1936.

GRIPPING TAIL

The cuscus has strong hands and feet and a powerful tail for moving around in rain forest trees. It is often mistaken for a monkey—but it's a marsupial.

HOLDING TIGHT

A koala's pouch opens at the bottom. Muscles inside hold the baby safe while the mother climbs trees.

INSECT EATERS

Moles, anteaters, hedgehogs, sloths, and shrews are all insect eaters. Most insect eaters have long, narrow noses to sniff out their dinner, and lots of small, sharp teeth. The giant anteater from Central and South America has no teeth at all. It has a long, worm-shaped tongue covered in sticky saliva, which it shoots out to lap up its favorite food—ants and termites. It can't see very well, but its sense of smell is at least 40 times more powerful than yours!

probing nose of a
Pyrenean desman

digging nose of
a European mole

NOSING AROUND
Animals that dig underground need sensitive noses to feel their prey. Long noses are good for probing under rocks.

short, bristly nose of
an Algerian hedgehog

SHAGGY RELATIVE

Sloths spend most of their time hanging upside down in forests. They eat leaves, but they belong to the same order as the giant anteater.

BATS

Bats are the only mammals that can truly fly. Some bats have wingspans as long as 5 feet (1.5 meters)! A bat wing is really a hand with long fingers that support the flight membrane, and a separate thumb with a claw. Most bats roost by hanging upside down in trees or caves. Some bats hunt frogs, fish, birds, and small mammals. Other bats sip nectar from fruit or flowers. The vampire bat has razor-sharp teeth, which it uses to slice open the skin of its animal prey—then it laps up the blood.

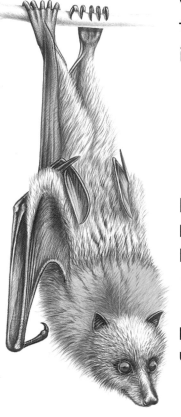

HANGING AROUND
Because a bat's front legs are part of its wings, they can't be used to hold on to a perch, so bats hang upside down instead!

BAT RADAR

Many bats hunt and navigate using echolocation, which is a bit like radar. The bat makes high-pitched sounds—too high for humans to hear—and then listens to how the sounds bounce off nearby objects.

THE DOG FAMILY

All dogs have strong, sharp teeth and good senses of sight, hearing, and smell. Wild dogs eat mainly meat, but also insects, fruit, and even snails. One species, the gray fox of North America, climbs trees in search of food. Many wild dogs are social mammals that live in groups. Most foxes live in pairs but often hunt alone. Wolves live and hunt in packs, working together to hunt and kill their prey. The adult wolves feed the cubs before eating their own meal.

Reading Faces
Coyotes use facial expressions to communicate.

Did You Know?
Wolf packs howl to tell other packs to stay away from their territory. They also howl to coordinate movements of a pack during a hunt.

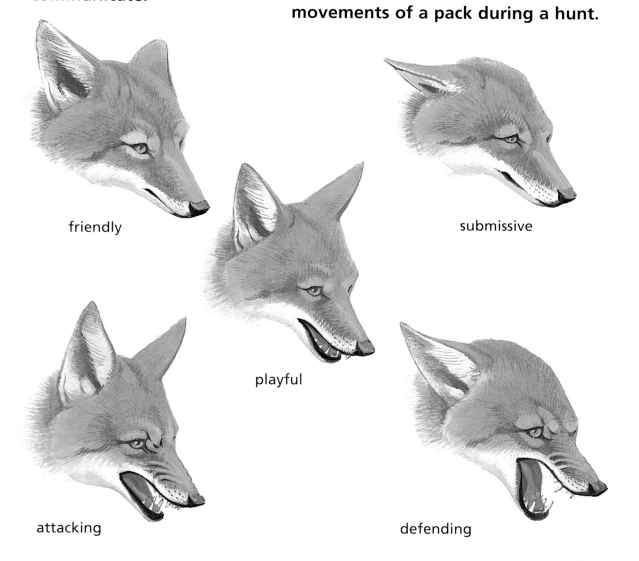

friendly

submissive

playful

attacking

defending

SMELLY MAMMALS

If you see an otter, a skunk, or a badger—beware! They belong to a family of meat-eating mammals that can let out a foul odor from a special scent gland. These smelly mammals are common almost everywhere in the world. They are rarely seen by humans because they live high in trees or hidden in burrows, and are often nocturnal, coming out only at night to search for food.

WHITE "BADGE"
A badger gets its name from the white mark on its head.

STRIPED WARNING

A skunk can fire foul-smelling liquid a great distance. Its black and white pattern warns predators to keep away.

AMAZING!

Sea otters sometimes use tools. To open a shell, a sea otter floats on its back, puts a rock on its stomach, and bangs the shell onto the rock.

RODENTS

Rodents have front teeth that are continually growing, ready for gnawing hard-shelled nuts, tree bark, or other plant food. Some rodents eat insects and other small animals as well as plants. Most rodents aren't very good at defending themselves, and they make easy prey for larger enemies. Many rodents have to produce large numbers of young to make sure their species survives.

capybara

lemming

crested porcupine

TYPES OF RODENTS

Some species of rodents might look similar, but their habits and behavior are very different.

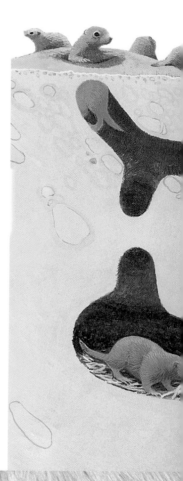

black rat

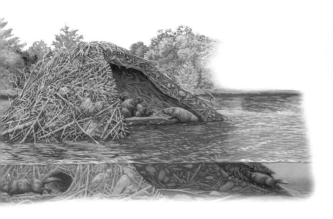

DID YOU KNOW?

Beavers build dams across rivers so that the water backs up to form a pond. In the middle of the pond, safe from predators, they build a nest called a lodge.

PRAIRIE DOG TOWN

Prairie dogs protect each other in huge underground towns. One town can cover 74 acres (30 hectares) and might house more than 1,000 animals.

FIGHTING FIT

Arctic hares chase each other around and have boxing matches in spring, to prove they'd be healthy mates.

BIG EARS

The jackrabbit lives in the desert. Its large ears help keep it cool during the day and also help it hear predators.

RABBITS AND HARES

Rabbits and hares are similar to rodents—they have front
teeth that are always growing. Because they also have
many predators, they have to give birth to lots of young
so that at least some survive. Rabbits and hares have
long ears, long front legs, and very long hind legs,
which they use to run and hop. European rabbits live
in burrows, called warrens, which protect them from
the weather and from predators.

IN THE TREE TOPS

Cotton-top tamarins are
New World monkeys from
Panama and Colombia.

DID YOU KNOW?

South American spider monkeys use their
tail like a fifth limb to hang on to
branches as they move about. Babies use
their tail to hang on to their mother.

Monkeys

There are two groups of monkeys. Old World monkeys live in Africa and Asia. They walk on all fours, and spend a lot of time on the ground. New World monkeys live in Central and South America, and spend most of their time in trees. Most New World monkeys have tails that can grip. If you can't tell whether a monkey is Old or New World, look at its nose. Old World monkeys have important-looking noses with nostrils that are close together and face forward. New World monkeys have flatter noses with nostrils that face sideways.

Hairy Howler
Male howler monkeys have shouting matches instead of fights. They can be heard nearly 2 miles (3.2 kilometers) away.

Nosing In
The proboscis monkey is an Old World monkey with a huge nose!

WHO'S THE BOSS?

In a lemur troop, the females are in charge of the males. They choose where to sit and get first pick of the food.

LEMURS

Lemurs live only on the African islands of Madagascar and Comoros. Their name comes from a Latin word for "ghost" because they cry eerily at night and have ghostly faces. Most lemurs live in wet forests, eating fruit, leaves, insects, and small animals such as geckos. After a cold night in the rain forest, ring-tailed lemurs stretch out in the trees and sunbathe before foraging for fruit and insects on the forest floor. All lemurs are endangered, because their forest habitat is being destroyed.

SAVE ME

The indri's back legs are much longer than its front legs, so on the ground, it has to hop! It is a very rare lemur and is now a protected species.

GLOSSARY

endangered In danger of becoming extinct.

evolved A description of a plant or animal whose body or habits have gradually changed in ways that allow it to live more successfully in its environment.

habitat The home of a plant or animal.

hibernate To have a long period of very deep sleep.

mammal An animal that grows inside its mother's body before it is born. The young drink their mother's milk.

marsupial A mammal that gives birth to young that are not fully developed. These young are protected in pouches.

membrane A thin, flexible tissue that connects parts of an animal.

monotreme A primitive mammal that lays eggs.

nocturnal A description of animals that sleep during the day and are active at night.

predators Animals that hunt and kill other animals.

prey Animals that are caught and eaten by other animals.

reptiles Cold-blooded animals that have backbones and dry skin covered by scales or a hard shell.

roost To settle down for rest or sleep.

INDEX

Picture and Illustration Credits

Books in This Series